D1032948

WITHDRAWN

DIGGING UP the Past

Ötzi The Iceman

Essential Library

An Imprint of Abdo Publishing | www.abdopublishing.com

-205 2219

DIGGING UP the Past

Ötzi
The Iceman

OCT 23 2014

CRANBERRY PUBLIC LIBRARY
2525 ROCHESTER ROAD, SUITE 300
CRANBERRY TOWNSHIP, PA 16066
724-776-9100

BY AMANDA LANSER

CONTENT CONSULTANT
DR. T. L. THURSTON, PROFESSOR,
DEPARTMENT OF ANTHROPOLOGY,
UNIVERSITY AT BUFFALO
STATE UNIVERSITY OF NEW YORK

www.abdopublishing.com

Published by Abdo Publishing, a division of ABDO, PO Box 398166, Minneapolis, Minnesota 55439. Copyright © 2015 by Abdo Consulting Group, Inc. International copyrights reserved in all countries. No part of this book may be reproduced in any form without written permission from the publisher. Essential Library™ is a trademark and logo of Abdo Publishing.

Printed in the United States of America, North Mankato, Minnesota
032014
092014

THIS BOOK CONTAINS
RECYCLED MATERIALS

Cover Photo: Südtiroler Museum/picture-alliance/dpa/AP Images
Interior Photos: Südtiroler Museum/picture-alliance/dpa/AP Images, 2; Vienna Report Agency/Sygma/Corbis, 6, 19, 21; Evgeny Eremeev/Shutterstock Images, 9; Red Line Editorial, 11, 35; Claus Felix/epa/Corbis, 12; Thinkstock, 15, 24, 35, 89; AFP/Getty Images, 22; Werner Nosko/epa/Corbis, 28; Andreas Fischer/AP Images, 32; Marka/SuperStock, 36, 57; Caro/Alamy, 41, 68, 86; Marco Albonico/Marka/SuperStock, 44; Gerhard Zwerger-Schoner/Glow Images, 49; Boris Kaulin/Thinkstock, 51; Samadelli Marco/EURAC/dpa/Corbis, 52, 82; Bernhard Grossruck/AP Images, 58; Shutterstock Images, 63; Bergelm Licht/Shutterstock Images, 65; Robert Parriger/epa/Corbis, 66, 73, 90; picture-alliance/dpa/AP Images, 75; Kazuhiko Sano/National Geographic Image Collection/ Glow Images, 77; Augustin Ochsenreiter-Archeological Museum of the Alto Adige/AP Images, 78; Bildagentur RM/Glow Images, 93; Petr David Josek/AP Images, 95; South Tyrol Museum of Archaeology/AP Images, 97

Editor: Lauren Coss
Series Designer: Becky Daum

Library of Congress Control Number: 2014932249

Cataloging-in-Publication Data

Lanser, Amanda.
 Otzi the iceman / Amanda Lanser.
  p. cm. -- (Digging up the past)
Includes bibliographical references and index.
ISBN 978-1-62403-235-6
1. Otzi (Ice mummy)--Juvenile literature. 2. Copper age--Italy--Hauslabjoch Pass--Juvenile literature. 3. Ice mummies--Italy--Hauslabjoch Pass--Juvenile literature.   4. Hauslabjoch Pass (Italy)--Antiquities--Juvenile literature. I. Title.
937--dc23
                                          2014932249

CONTENTS

1

A Glimpse into the Past

On September 19, 1991, Erika and Helmut Simon, a German couple, were hiking down a peak in the Alps, a major European mountain range. They had spent the last day and a half trekking through a portion of the range that defines the Italian-Austrian border. Now they were trudging down the trail toward town. At approximately noon, Helmut spotted something sticking out of the snow and ice on the side of the mountain. He turned away from

In 1991, the body of an ancient, mummified man was discovered in the Alps on the border of Austria and Italy. The man was nicknamed Ötzi.

the object, disgusted. Another hiker had decided to dump trash on the mountain, he thought.

However, Erika gave the object a more careful look. After a moment, she yelled down the trail to Helmut, "Look! It's a person!"[1] This discovery would set in motion archaeological and scientific research that continues today.

AN ANCIENT HUMAN

After some investigation, scientists determined the body the Simons discovered was more than 5,000 years old. This made it the oldest intact remains of a modern human ever found. The body was no mere

THE ÖTZTAL ALPS

Ötzi was found in the part of the Alps that serve as the border between Austria and Italy. On the Austrian side is a 40-mile- (64 km) long valley called the Ötztal Valley.[2] The Ötztal Alps is a popular tourist destination for Europeans. It has some of the highest skiing in Austria and luxurious spas where skiers can go to relax after hitting the slopes. At more than 10,000 feet (3,000 m) tall, the mountains where Ötzi was found are inhospitable environments, with snow and ice much of the year.[3] Few humans would have lived there during Ötzi's lifetime, though now several ski resorts dot their ridges.

skeleton. It had been mummified. Glacial ice had preserved it for thousands of years, leaving skin, hands, feet, internal organs, and even eyeballs intact. Researchers began calling the mummy Ötzi (UHT-zee) after the Ötztal Alps where he was found. Others gave the mummy the nickname "Iceman." Ötzi's body and the artifacts found with him would become the subject of numerous studies and tests for years to come.

Ötzi is a unique archaeological find. Unlike other archaeological digs that focus on a particular location, Ötzi's body *is* the archaeological dig. For more than 20 years, the Iceman has continued offering a wealth of information about how he lived and died. Scientists have to be careful to preserve the body for future study. Every bit

The snow-capped beauty of the Ötztal Alps attracts skiers and hikers.

of tissue or piece of artifact is precious. Scientists take preserving the body and the artifacts very seriously.

The study of the Iceman has given scientists the opportunity to use new technologies and even invent new ones. These new technologies help scientists understand Ötzi's world and what late Stone Age humans were like. They also help advance the science of archaeology and the tools available to archaeologists around the world.

Ötzi's remains and the artifacts found with him give scientists and people around the world a better understanding of the Neolithic period of history. His remains show scientists how humans lived thousands of years ago. The Iceman offers modern

THE NEOLITHIC PERIOD

The late period of the Stone Age is known as the Neolithic period. In Europe, it lasted from approximately 7000 to 2500 BCE. The Iceman lived during the very end of the Neolithic period. During the Neolithic period, humans in Asia, the Middle East, and Europe used advanced stone tools. During the previous era, the Mesolithic era, humans had domesticated certain plants. This allowed them to grow crops for food rather than gathering plants and berries to eat. Agriculture turned nomadic, or traveling, societies into communities that stayed put on an area of land. Farming was much more common during the Neolithic period than in past eras of history.

humans a look into the distant past. He lived during a time without kings or countries. Furthermore, artifacts found with Ötzi revolutionized scientists' understanding of the technological advancements of the late Stone Age. The Iceman gave people around the world a new appreciation for the intellect and capabilities of ancient humans.

WHERE IS ÖTZI?

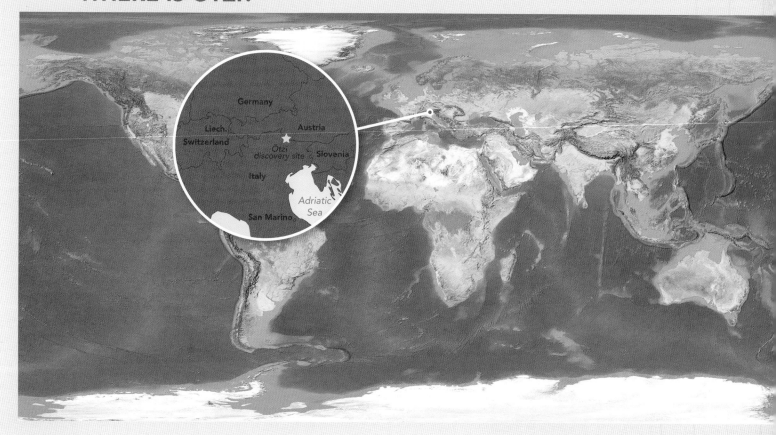

VERÖFFENTLICHUNGEN
DER
UNIVERSITÄT INNSBRUCK
187

DER MANN IM EIS
Band 1

Bericht über das Internationale Symposium 1992 in Innsbruck

2

Discovery and Recovery

Helmut and Erika Simon began their fateful hike in late September 1991. Although the season was just changing over from summer to fall, the summits of the Alps along the Austrian-Italian border were covered in glacial ice and snow. One of these peaks, Similaun, reached more than 11,800 feet (3,600 m) into the sky.[1] Its sides were covered in deep trenches in the ice called crevasses. The experienced hikers were slowed by the crevasses. A single misstep

German hikers Erika and Helmut Simon were the first humans to lay eyes on Ötzi in thousands of years.

THE ALPS

Ötzi was discovered in one of the most iconic mountain ranges in the world. The Alps run from the south coast of France through Switzerland, Italy, and Austria and then on into Eastern Europe, finally ending in Albania. The mountain range covers approximately 80,000 square miles (207,000 sq km). Where the mountains reach more than 5,000 feet (1,500 m) tall, as where Ötzi was found, winter snowfalls can drop 10 to 33 feet (3 to 10 m) of snow.[2] With that kind of severe weather, it is no surprise Ötzi was buried under ice and snow for more than 5,000 years.

would swallow them up without hope of being rescued.

Despite these treacherous conditions, the Simons continued toward the summit. The couple had planned to climb up and then back down Similaun in a single day, but the dangerous trail conditions made that goal impossible. After reaching the top of the peak, Helmut and Erika decided to stay overnight in a hikers' lodge on the mountain. At the lodge, the Simons met a couple from Austria who invited them to climb to the summit of another mountain the next day. Early the next morning, on September 19, 1991, both couples set out to climb to the top of Finail Peak.

The two couples made it to the top of Finail Peak, and after taking pictures, said their good-byes and took different trails down the mountain. The Austrian couple turned down a path toward the Ötztal Valley, while the Simons headed back down toward their lodge. They were soon delayed because their path was partly blocked with melting snow and ice. Instead of finding another trail down from the summit, Helmut led the way around the melting snow and ice. By taking this minor detour, the Simons stumbled upon one of the most fascinating archaeological finds in the world.

JUST ANOTHER PIECE OF TRASH

On the summit of Finail Peak, Helmut had been disgusted when he noticed several pieces of broken glass from a champagne bottle summer tourists had left behind. Now, along the trail back to the lodge, he spotted something sticking out of the snow ahead of him. Helmut assumed the object was just another piece of trash left behind by a careless tourist.

A moment later, however, both he and Erika realized what they were seeing. It was a human body, lying half-buried in

The European Alps run for 750 miles (1,200 km) from the Mediterranean Sea to central Austria.

CRANBERRY PUBLIC LIBRARY
2525 ROCHESTER ROAD, SUITE 300
CRANBERRY TOWNSHIP, PA 16066
724-776-9100

the snow. The body was facedown, and from what the Simons could tell, it was naked from the waist up. The corpse was bald and shrunken. The couple inched closer to the body. They saw the person had suffered a severe blow to the head, which had left a massive wound on the back of his or her skull. When Erika and Helmut looked around the body, they found some birch bark wound with leather laces. Erika thought perhaps a bird had made the contraption.

The couple decided to continue down the mountain toward the lodge. They thought the body was that of an unfortunate hiker or mountain climber. That night, they reported the body to the lodge's caretaker, Markus Pirpamer. Pirpamer had grown up on the mountain. He was the son of the head volunteer of an Austrian village's Alpine rescue team. When the Simons told him they had found a body, Pirpamer asked them where the body was and what condition it was in. He told the Simons he would handle reporting the body to the police. Pirpamer knew deciding which police to call—the Austrians or the Italians—would be tricky. Even though he was very familiar with Finail Peak, he was not able to immediately determine if the body lay in Italy or Austria. Pirpamer decided to call both the gendarmes in the town of Sölden, Austria, and the carabinieri in the Schnalstal Valley of Italy.

After making phone calls to both authorities, Pirpamer ventured out to locate the body. He found the corpse as the Simons had described it—facedown in the snow, naked from the waist up, and with a serious wound to the back of the head. Pirpamer's keen eye also spotted several objects around the body. He found the hide of a chamois, a goatlike mammal native to the Alps; an ax with a wooden handle and a metal blade; and what seemed to be a long, whittled wooden walking stick. He also spotted the birch bark bound with leather strips the Simons had discovered. After taking a final look around the site, Pirpamer headed back to the lodge.

A DIFFICULT RECOVERY

Meanwhile, the Italian carabinieri were trying to determine in which country the body lay. They did not have access to an official map of the border region, so they used the best available map of the area, which was a map designed for area tourists. The carabinieri decided the corpse was in Austrian territory. The gendarmes in Sölden, Austria, used the same tourist map to determine where the corpse lay. They also decided the body was under their jurisdiction.

LEAVING THE STONE AGE, ENTERING THE BRONZE AGE

Approximately 5,000 years ago, the Neolithic period of the Stone Age ended and the Bronze Age began. During the Bronze Age, humans developed a way to melt and use metal to make tools and weapons. Copper was the first metal ancient humans used. One of the artifacts found with Ötzi was a copper-headed ax. Scientists were surprised to find a metal-headed tool with such an old mummy. The tool helped them place Ötzi's life between the Neolithic period and the Bronze Age.

GENDARMES AND CARABINIERI

Gendarme is a French word for an armed police officer. Other countries have adopted the word to describe their own armed police forces. Austrian gendarmes are responsible for policing rural areas of the country, including the towns and villages in the Alps. In Italy, carabinieri are members of the country's national police force. They not only perform national police duties but also work with other countries on international security concerns.

The next day, on Friday, September 20, 1991, the Austrian gendarmes sent Anton Koler, a regional inspector from the Ötztal Valley, to recover the body. Koler took a helicopter to the site, where he met Pirpamer. Pirpamer led him to the body, and the two men attempted to dig it out. Half of the body was still stuck in the ice, and Pirpamer and Koler had a difficult time removing it. Koler had brought a small jackhammer that ran on compressed air. Koler and Pirpamer used the jackhammer to chip away at the ice surrounding the body. The men soon discovered the corpse was draped over a large boulder. The body's left arm was crossed under its chest, and its right arm hung down into the ice. The body's placement made it difficult for Koler to get a good angle on the ice. He hit the body a few times with the tip of the jackhammer, tearing the skin. After about an hour, the jackhammer's compressed air ran out, and the weather turned threatening. The men decided to leave the corpse exposed, still stuck in the ice, but they took the ax Pirpamer had spotted the day before with them.

Koler and Pirpamer spent the next day attempting to dig out the body with no success. They covered the corpse with a plastic tarp, so it was not visible to hikers trekking to and from the Finail Peak summit. Over the next few days, a number of mountaineers and locals headed up to the peak to look for artifacts and see the body. Several tried to remove the body, but all attempts were unsuccessful.

On Monday, September 23, a reporter from the Austrian television

Because of the frozen conditions surrounding the Iceman, digging the body out proved more challenging than officials had anticipated.

network Ötsterreichischer Rundfunk (ORF) flew up to the site by helicopter to film the rest of the recovery. On the way up to the site, the helicopter picked up Pirpamer, who was able to direct the pilot on where to land. Soon, a second helicopter landed with a two-man recovery crew from the Austrian government. Professor of forensics Rainer Henn of Innsbruck University in Austria and Austrian gendarme Roman Lukasser worked with an ice pick and ski pole to clear the ice and snow from the corpse. Eventually, the ice gave way, and the men were able to see for the first time what the corpse's face looked like. The corpse's eyes and mouth were both open, and Professor Henn observed that the body was partly mummified. He and Lukasser placed the corpse facedown in a body bag and continued analyzing the area around where the body had been.

CAMERA-SHY ÖTZI

One notable thing about the discovery and recovery of Ötzi is a lack of photographic evidence of the site. When Inspector Koler arrived on the scene, he did not believe the body was involved in any sort of crime. Instead of taking dozens of photographs of the scene, including documentation of where the body lay and the location of surrounding artifacts, he only took two—one each of the corpse and the artifacts. In fact, no one else took photos or film of the scene until the camera crew from ORF arrived at the site during the last day of recovery efforts.

After freeing Ötzi from the ice, officials moved his body to Innsbruck University for research.

After some digging with the ice pick and the ski pole, Henn and Lukasser found a small knife with a blade made of stone. They also discovered a grass mat draped on a boulder and a small bit of leather. The men managed to extract the long, whittled stick Pirpamer had noticed out of the ice, although they had to break the stick to do so. In all, it only took the team approximately 70 minutes to remove the body and the rest of the artifacts from the side of the mountain.[3] The team flew the body in a helicopter to Vent, Austria, where it was placed in a wooden coffin and taken to the Institute of Forensic Medicine at Innsbruck University. There, scientists quickly realized the body some had thought was a lost hiker was in fact thousands of years old.

3

Early Work

The Italians first gave jurisdiction over Ötzi to the Austrians. However, shortly after his body was recovered, Italian officials began arguing the Iceman had in fact been found on Italian soil. Both Italian and Austrian authorities understood the importance of determining which country Ötzi belonged to. It was more than just a matter of where the body would reside for research. Both Italy and Austria saw the potential the Iceman had in connecting people with their history and traditions, which would lead

A photo of Ötzi, taken on September 24, 1991, shows the contorted position his body was found in.

to an increase in tourism. On October 2, 1991, an official survey of the area determined Ötzi had indeed been found on Italian soil, just 303 feet (92 m) from the border between Italy and Austria.[1]

The survey affirmed Italy's claim to the mummy. However, the corpse was already in the possession of scientists at Austria's Innsbruck University. A compromise was reached. The province of South Tyrol, on the Italian side of the border, would be the real owner of the body, but the mummy would stay in Innsbruck for research. In a show of good faith, the governor of South Tyrol allowed researchers from the university to continue studying the site where Ötzi was found.

Ötzi's first home after being recovered was in the Alpine town of Innsbruck, Austria.

The Innsbruck University team was thrilled to be leading the research on Ötzi. No body as ancient and intact as Ötzi's had been found before. The team was eager to discover what secrets the Iceman and his artifacts would reveal. A few days after the recovery crews removed Ötzi from the mountainside, Andreas Lippert and his team of researchers arrived at the recovery site by helicopter. Lippert was part of the Department of Prehistory and Early History at Innsbruck University. At the site, he and his team met Konrad Spindler, head of the department. Lippert would perform an emergency excavation on the site where Ötzi had been found. Lippert's team would try to plot the site, thoroughly investigate the area around the boulder where the body had lain, and search for more artifacts.

Lippert and his team had some hard work ahead of them. Two feet (0.6 m) of fresh snow had fallen before the scientists were able to start their excavation.[2] When the site was cleared, the team realized the many people who had visited the site since its discovery

"You know, the scientist does not like to take words like 'great moment,' 'hundred-year find,' or other superlatives in his mouth, but in this case it appears really justified that even the dry scientist gets a little excited and lets himself reach for words that do not belong to his usual vocabulary."[3]

—KONRAD SPINDLER ON ÖTZI'S DISCOVERY

had disturbed it badly. Artifacts had been moved or removed, and no photographs of the original scene had been taken. This made it difficult for Lippert and his team to understand the context of the few artifacts they recovered. What little they did find was often damaged, including objects such as Ötzi's shoes and clothing. The team also found evidence of the forceful extraction of Ötzi's body from the ice. Before Lippert's team could thoroughly investigate the site, however, persistent snow kept covering key dig areas. Despite these setbacks, by the end of their excavation, Lippert and his team had found 5,000-year-old maple leaves, a grass net, two pieces of animal bone, bits of fur and leather, and what appeared to be a grass mat frozen onto the boulder.

MARKUS EGG

Soon after Ötzi was found, several artifacts had been transported to the lab of Markus Egg. Egg was a conservator at the Roman-Germanic Central Museum in Austria. He was responsible for taking an inventory of all the items found with the Iceman and documenting the artifacts for future scientists' reference and study. He was also charged with conserving the artifacts. Since the artifacts were kept in Egg's lab, he had control over when other researchers were able to study the artifacts. Egg only allowed the artifacts to be studied after his team had studied, photographed, cleaned, repaired, preserved, and documented each one. This system helped Egg keep track of the artifacts and record the condition in which they were found.

Egg was very familiar with Stone Age artifacts from other locations across Europe. However, few ancient objects from the Ötztal Valley had been found or studied before. Egg had grown up in the region, and he had learned about the area's prehistory from his father, who also studied prehistoric humans. This background helped him analyze Ötzi's artifacts and make logical inferences about his life and times.

ÖTZI'S WEAPONS

Egg's first task was to analyze the long, narrow stick found with Ötzi. Egg determined the stick was a bow. At the time, the bow was one of only a few of its age known to exist anywhere in the world. Even though it was broken at one end, Egg believed the bow had been shaped like a *D*. It would have stood approximately as tall as a man. There were small whittling marks up and down the surface of the bow. Egg was not surprised Ötzi's discoverers had first thought the bow was a walking stick since there was no bowstring. However, Egg was surprised to find there

MIMICKING NATURE

To conserve Ötzi's artifacts, Egg used a conservation method that kept the objects wet, mimicking the glacial conditions in which they were found. Instead of using chemicals to preserve the artifacts, Egg placed them each in a water bath, where they would stay for a year. After this long soak, the objects were dried out slowly and then wrapped in plastic.

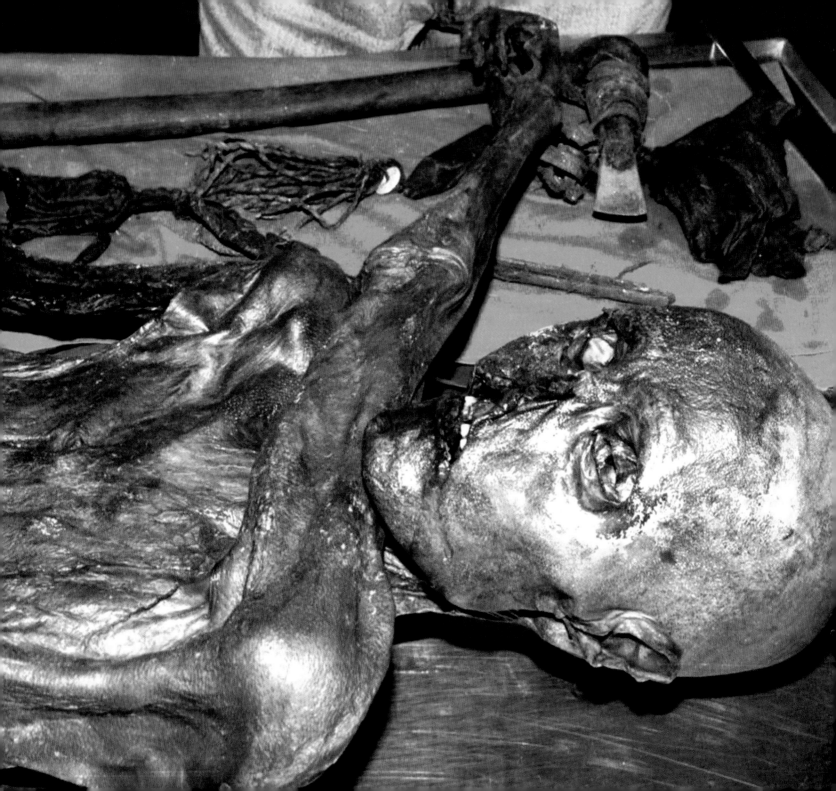

was no place to attach a string to the bow. This led him to infer the bow was unfinished. After making these discoveries, Egg placed the bow in a water bath, the first step in the conservation process.

Egg moved on to the Iceman's unusual ax. He noticed the blade was heavy and had a dull edge, perhaps from frequent use. It was possible Ötzi had used the ax to make the bow Egg had just examined. What impressed Egg the most about the weapon was the way its maker had crafted it. The handle was created from a piece of wood that came from the part of a tree where the trunk had met a large branch. This would have made it a strong, hefty piece of timber. Then, the maker had put a notch in the branch end where the blade would rest. The blade was attached to the wooden handle with a substance Egg believed was tree pitch. The blade was then secured with leather strips.

Another weapon found with Ötzi was a flint-bladed dagger. During his analysis, Egg noted the flint blade was approximately three inches (8 cm) long.[4] The blade was fastened to a handle made of ash wood. Egg also determined the blade appeared to have been well used. Its edge was worn from frequent sharpening, which created serrations along the blade. Egg's

The artifacts discovered with Ötzi provide important insight into the Iceman's lifestyle.

analysis of Ötzi's weapons was slowly revealing new information about prehistoric humans living in the Alps.

CONSERVING THE ICEMAN

While Egg was able to use established conservation techniques on the Iceman's artifacts, the scientist tasked with preserving Ötzi was not so fortunate. After he was extracted from the ice, Ötzi was sent to the lab of Werner Platzer, the head of Innsbruck University's Anatomy Department. Platzer's lab was the only facility at the university with freezers large enough to house the Iceman. But Platzer was not sure of the best way to preserve the corpse. Ötzi was a wet, natural mummy, meaning he had been preserved by nature in a wet environment, unlike Egyptian mummies, which were prepared for burial by humans and then placed in tombs in the desert. This meant Ötzi had retained some humidity. If Platzer failed to find a way to preserve this humidity, the Iceman would dry out and fall apart.

After some thought, Platzer decided to keep Ötzi's freezer just under 32 degrees Fahrenheit (0°C) and at 70 percent relative humidity.[5] These were the conditions he had used to preserve other human tissue samples he had previously studied. Platzer hoped to preserve the Iceman in conditions that were as close as possible to those in which he was found. At these levels,

Platzer believed Ötzi's corpse, including dried blood in his heart and food and parasites in his gut, would be preserved and available for study.

END-OF-YEAR DISCOVERY

In early December 1991, radiocarbon dating of grass samples taken from the site where Ötzi was found was complete. Spindler was surprised at the results. The Iceman was approximately 1,000 years older than the 4,000 years Spindler had initially estimated. The radiocarbon dating determined Ötzi had been alive approximately 5,300 years ago.

Spindler and Egg took another look at Ötzi's ax. Spindler believed the ax head was made of bronze, but conventional thinking about

WHAT IS RELATIVE HUMIDITY?

Determining an appropriate relative humidity was vitally important to Ötzi's preservation. For every unit of temperature, there is a maximum amount of possible humidity, or amount of water vapor in the atmosphere. Relative humidity is the ratio of the humidity actually present in the atmosphere compared to the maximum possible humidity. Relative humidity is expressed as a percentage. Platzer decided to keep the Iceman at 70 percent humidity, or at a level that equaled 70 percent of the greatest amount of humidity possible for the temperature in the freezer.

KONRAD SPINDLER

Konrad Spindler knew the Simons' discovery on the mountain was special even before he first laid eyes on the Iceman. He had been following news about the discovery after he saw a report regarding Ötzi's unusual ax. Because of Spindler's experience as a historical archaeologist, he knew the ax meant Ötzi was someone special. Axes were often status symbols in ancient times. When Spindler got the opportunity to investigate the body, he jumped at it.

Spindler was the first archaeologist to see Ötzi. He quickly assumed the lead in Ötzi's research, also raising awareness and money for future study of the mummy. In 1993, he was one of the first scientists to present a theory on how Ötzi died.

Austrian archaeologist Konrad Spindler was one of the key researchers involved in studying the Iceman.

prehistoric humans claimed humans did not learn how to make bronze until 1,000 years after the Iceman's death. Egg analyzed the metal blade. He found the blade was nearly pure copper. This was a very exciting find. The discovery prompted a complete rethinking of the timeline of technological advancement in the Alpine region. Prior to Egg's analysis, scientists believed humans during Ötzi's time relied on stone tools. The copper ax's design was more advanced than scientists thought possible. Just three months after his discovery, the Iceman was already making waves in the archaeological world.

DIGGING
DEEPER

Radiocarbon Dating

Radiocarbon dating is a technique scientists use to date organic material, including bone, wood, charcoal, and even cloth. Scientists first take a sample of the material to be dated and measure the amount of radioactive carbon, called carbon-14 or C-14, present in the specimen. C-14 is found in the atmosphere and absorbed by plants during photosynthesis. When animals eat plants, they absorb the C-14 from the plants. Once the plant or animal dies, the amount of C-14 in the organism starts to decay. Scientists measure this decay by measuring the half-life of carbon. An element's half-life is the time it takes for one-half of that element to decay. The half-life of carbon is 5,730 years. By determining the amount of C-14 still present in a sample, scientists can

The Decay of Carbon-14

0 years	5,730 years	11,460 years	17,190 years

C-14 atoms

C-14 decay

C-14 absorbed by plants

discover how old the sample material is. Radiocarbon dating is a helpful tool for many archaeologists and other scientists.

4

Research Continues

While archaeologists made a lot of progress in the few months following Ötzi's discovery, study of the mummy and his belongings was just getting started. For example, Egg's work with Ötzi's artifacts did not end with the mummy's weapons. He was also responsible for the conservation of the Iceman's other belongings.

By studying Ötzi's artifacts, researchers have been able to put together a picture of how the Iceman may have used them and what he may have looked like.

UNDERSTANDING ÖTZI'S CLOTHING

Some of the most intriguing artifacts were the leather bits and scraps found alongside Ötzi. Egg and his assistant, Roswitha Goedecker-Ciolek, were determined to understand these artifacts. The leather pieces were so brittle the scientists had to soak them in an oily bath and rinse them with distilled water before handling them. During this reconditioning process, Goedecker-Ciolek observed that some of the pieces had fur attached to them. Upon closer inspection, she discovered a tiny piece of grain stuck in the fur of one of the scraps. She called Egg over to take a look,

CONSERVING ÖTZI

Ötzi's artifacts were not the only things scientists were concerned about conserving. Scientists continued honing the technique they used to conserve Ötzi's body. While Platzer's temperature and relative humidity levels were maintained, scientists developed an effective, though labor-intensive, process for preserving the mummy.

First, Ötzi was wrapped in a sterile cloth, covered in ice, and laid on a foam pad. Then, alternating layers of plastic sheeting and ice were wrapped around Ötzi. The mummy took approximately five minutes to unwrap. To maintain a sterile environment, new sheets were required every time the body was uncovered. In 1992, Innsbruck University invested in two new freezers just for Ötzi, with eight sensors monitoring the temperature and humidity levels.[1]

and he immediately became excited. His trained eye knew the grain was domesticated. It meant Ötzi's community knew how to grow crops for food. In a few days, analysis of that grain and another found soon after revealed the seeds were from a domesticated crop called einkorn, an ancient form of wheat. Egg called Spindler to tell him the news.

Meanwhile, Goedecker-Ciolek continued her work with Ötzi's leather scraps. She observed the leather scraps were often composed of several different kinds of hides sewn together. As she tried to piece together the scraps, she realized she had uncovered Ötzi's clothing. Some pieces looked like the sleeves of a shirt or pant legs, while another piece was the size of a beach towel and had strips of alternating dark and light fur.

After further study, Goedecker-Ciolek realized the sleeve-shaped scraps were actually leggings designed to cover the Iceman's legs from midcalf to midthigh. The leggings would have been secured to another scrap of cloth, which Egg and Goedecker-Ciolek determined was a loincloth. These leggings would have provided some warmth for Ötzi in the cool Alpine

EARLY CROP: EINKORN

Einkorn was one of the first domesticated plants in the Alps. The grain grows well in the soils of the Alpine valleys where Ötzi likely lived. Scientists believe Ötzi could have eaten the grain whole or ground up into flour for hard, cracker-like bread. Einkorn still grows wild in the Ötztal Valley region. Although it is rarely grown today, domestic einkorn is gaining popularity as a health food.

climate. The beach towel–shaped scrap was more puzzling. Goedecker-Ciolek knew the piece was well worn because she found evidence of sweat and discoloration. However, she had not recovered any sleeves. Goedecker-Ciolek inferred that Ötzi wore the large scrap on his torso. However, she and Egg could not find evidence showing how Ötzi kept the garment on his body.

Goedecker-Ciolek also studied the grass mat Lippert's team found on the side of the boulder. She decided it was actually a large cape. She noticed the top half of the mat was woven, while the bottom half was not, so the grasses hung freely like a hula skirt. This design would have reached past Ötzi's knees and probably allowed him to move about freely while keeping warm under the cape.

The last pieces of the puzzle surrounding Ötzi's clothing were his shoes. The Iceman wore primitive shoes with leather soles and grass uppers that formed a net. The shoes were stuffed with more grass for insulation against the harsh mountain climate. After further study, Goedecker-Ciolek discovered that a tiny tab of fur inside the shoe matched a similar tab of fur stuck to the leggings. These tabs would have allowed Ötzi to secure his shoes to his leggings to keep out the snow and cold.

Goedecker-Ciolek suspected that some of the leather scraps had originally come from domesticated animals. A year after her work began, her hunch would be partially confirmed by Willy Groenman-Van Waateringe, a scientist from the Netherlands. He had analyzed bits of Goedecker-Ciolek's scraps to identify the types of animals from which they came. He found Ötzi's loincloth was made from the hide of a goat, a domesticated animal. Ötzi's cape and leggings were made from red deer hide. His shoes were made of bearskin and red deer hides.

OEGGL'S ILLUMINATING DISCOVERY

In December 1991, Egg delivered the leaves found with Ötzi to Klaus Oeggl's lab for analysis. Oeggl was an assistant botany professor at Innsbruck University. He was a paleobotanist,

A replica of the Iceman's leggings can be seen at a museum in Umhausen, Austria.

which meant his expertise was in studying fossilized and ancient plants. He saw Ötzi as a rare opportunity to advance the paleobotany field. Oeggl set to work to discover what Egg's sample would reveal about Ötzi's life. Slowly, Oeggl separated what would turn out to be 14 layers of maple leaves stacked together like the pages of a book. All the leaves were missing their stems.

After soaking bits of the leaves in alcohol, Oeggl took a look at the bits under a microscope. What he found surprised him. There was still chlorophyll present in the 5,300-year-old leaves, a sign the leaves were living when Ötzi plucked them from a tree.

Among the leaves, Oeggl found tiny bits of charcoal, pine needles, and birch bark. Oeggl shared his findings with Egg, who suspected Ötzi may have used the leaf package to keep the embers of a fire warm. This would have made it easier for him to start fires while traveling. Oeggl further analyzed the tiny charcoal pieces and found they were from trees that grew farther down the mountain than where Ötzi was discovered. This suggested he had spent time in the lower altitudes of the surrounding valleys not long before his death.

CONTAINING FIRE

Ötzi could have used his little packet of charcoal wrapped carefully in maple leaves to carry an ember from a dying fire with him to his next campsite. Once there, he could add some twigs and reignite it. This technique is not unique to Ötzi or the area in which he lived. When discussing the findings with Oeggl, Egg remembered reading about the same kind of practice among Native Americans.

LIPPERT'S SECOND DIG

In July 1992, Lippert and his team of archaeologists conducted another dig at the site where Ötzi was found. Even though it was midsummer, the team still faced poor weather conditions. The temperature was as low as 36 degrees Fahrenheit (2°C), and there was 660 short tons (600 metric tons) of snow to remove before Lippert's team could get to work.[2] During the dig, both accumulating snow and snowmelt slowed the team's efforts. They did not want to miss any piece of information at the site, so all snowmelt runoff was filtered through mesh before being allowed to leave the site. This practice helped Lippert's team uncover some small but interesting artifacts, including a fingernail.

Lippert's second dig lasted five weeks and uncovered 400 objects the team believed were related to the Iceman. One of these artifacts was the rest of Ötzi's bow, which was still stuck in the ice from when the recovery team had broken it off the year before. Like the other piece of the bow Egg had studied and documented, the piece Lippert's team recovered did not show any evidence that it had been strung. Another interesting find Lippert and his team uncovered was a fur cap. The bowl-shaped hat was found near the boulder, which caused Lippert to infer it must have fallen off Ötzi's head at some point. One year after the dig, Groenman-Van Waateringe, the

Researchers were able to recreate Ötzi's bearskin cap.

Dutch scientist who analyzed Goedecker-Ciolek's leather scraps, found the cap was made of bear fur.

In addition to the piece of bow and cap, the team collected bits of organic matter for botanists to analyze, including plant matter, mud, hair, and even water and ice from the site. These specimens were delivered to Oeggl for analysis.

SOLVING THE MYSTERY OF ÖTZI'S DEATH

Dieter zur Nedden was a radiologist at Innsbruck University when Ötzi was discovered. He was responsible for taking X-ray images of Ötzi's skeleton and internal organs and analyzing them for evidence of how Ötzi may have died. Zur Nedden's X-rays uncovered evidence of trauma. The Iceman had several broken ribs on both sides of his torso. The breaks on the left side showed evidence of healing, which meant they had been broken during Ötzi's lifetime. However, fractures on some of Ötzi's other ribs revealed no evidence of healing. Zur Nedden hypothesized that these breaks must have occurred after the Iceman died or shortly before he died, before the bones had a chance to begin the healing process.

Zur Nedden also took computed tomography (CT) scan images of Ötzi's body, which allowed him to look inside the mummy. The images revealed Ötzi's brain had shrunk down to the size of an orange over the last 5,300 years. The Iceman also had hardened arteries,

WHAT IS A CT SCAN?

Imagine a loaf of sliced bread. Each slice fits snugly with its neighbors to make up the loaf. You can leave the slices together to see the entire loaf, or take one of the slices out to look at the inside of the loaf. A CT scan works a bit like a loaf of bread. It takes X-ray images of an entire body and creates cross-sectioned images, similar to bread slices, so doctors and scientists can study the inside of the body. The images help doctors and scientists look at bones, muscles, organs, and other things that may be inside a body.

conservators. During the meeting, the experts were able to view the mummy and learn about the research conducted so far. The experts would then be able to provide feedback on their peers' research, which would allow Ötzi's researchers to develop their theories further. Attendees also listened to a presentation from Spindler titled "The Iceman's Last Weeks." In the presentation, Spindler explained his theory on how Ötzi had died.

Spindler's theory was based on the idea that Ötzi was a herdsman. In his presentation, Spindler described a scenario in which the Iceman was up in the mountains tending a herd of animals. Around the time of his death, which Spindler believed was in early fall, Ötzi was bringing the herd down from the mountain for the winter. When he made it to his community, Spindler asserted, Ötzi fell victim to some sort of violence, possibly an attack. Though he was injured by the violence and his equipment damaged, Ötzi fled to the mountains, where he spent a few days or even weeks. Eventually, the Iceman found shelter against a rock, where he ate some meat. Lippert's team had found some animal bones close to the boulder, which supported this idea. After eating, the herdsman perished from the cold.

Similaun Peak, where Ötzi's body was first found and where Spindler believed the Iceman met his end

> "[Ötzi] knew that sleep meant death. . . . With his last ounce of strength he turned himself onto his left side, the least painful position for his injured rib cage. Then he fell into the sleep from which he was to awaken no more. Snow covered his body."[4]
>
> —KONRAD SPINDLER, PRESENTING HIS THEORY ON ÖTZI'S DEATH AT A 1993 CONFERENCE

A MUMMY WITH TATTOOS

By late 1993, Ötzi's body had been studied inside and out and the excavation site had been thoroughly examined. However, that did not mean there was nothing left to discover. Ötzi had several tattoo-like markings on his skin. Norwegian anthropologist Torstein Sjøvold took a closer look at the markings to determine their significance.

Sjøvold used an infrared light to study 14 different tattoos found all over Ötzi's body.[5] The tattoos were sets of vertical lines situated over the Iceman's anklebones, calves, knees, and back. The tattoos were the color of charcoal, leading scientists to believe they were made with soot. Analyzing the tattoos, Sjøvold realized they always appeared on areas of the Iceman's body that likely caused him pain, such as his joints and his back. Sjøvold hypothesized that Ötzi had used the tattoos as a type of therapy for the arthritis zur Nedden's images had uncovered. The tattoos were likely an early form of acupuncture, which is an ancient Chinese pain-relief technique that involves

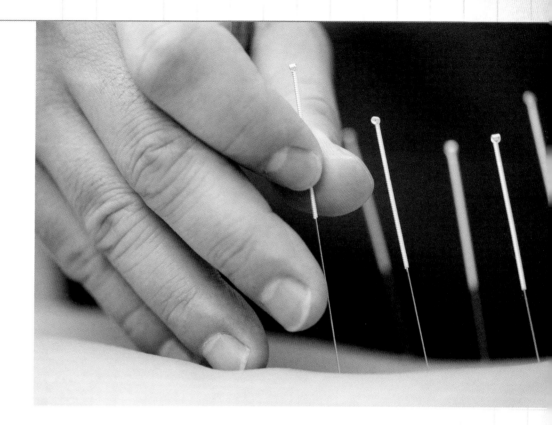

Some scientists think Ötzi's tattoos may have been used to relieve pain, similar to acupuncture.

inserting small needles at various pressure points in the body. However, Ötzi's tattoos were 2,000 years older than when scientists believed Asian acupuncture had originated.

The research conducted in 1992 and 1993 helped scientists begin to understand who Ötzi was and the time in which he lived. However, as technology improved, there was still plenty of information for scientists to discover.

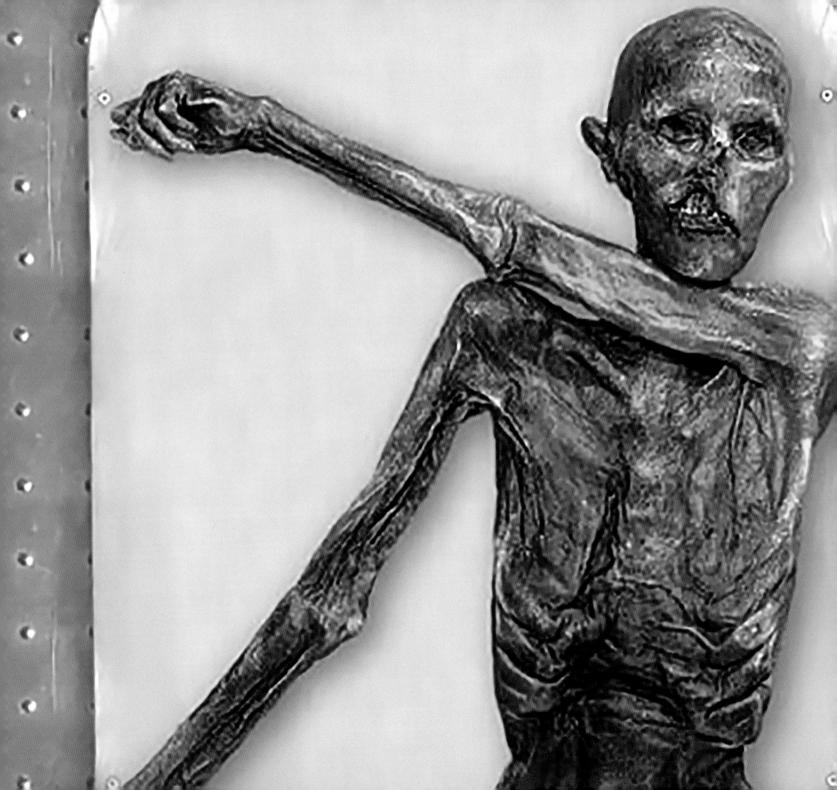

5

A Move to Italy

Research on Ötzi continued uncovering surprising finds. But work on the food contents of Ötzi's digestive tract had not been thoroughly investigated. In 1991, X-ray images taken by radiologist zur Nedden had led scientists to believe there was something in Ötzi's colon to study. The colon is an organ that is part of the lower digestive tract, so anything found in it would help scientists understand what the Iceman ate. Late one night in 1996, Oeggl took out a tiny specimen of Ötzi's colon

The more scientists studied Ötzi, the more exciting discoveries they made.

contents. The sample was approximately the size of a human fingernail. Though Oeggl's sample was miniscule, his keen eye was able to uncover a trove of information under the microscope.

ELECTRON MICROSCOPES

Like regular microscopes used in science classes, electron microscopes are used to study tiny objects and organisms invisible to the naked eye. However, unlike a regular microscope, which uses light, electron microscopes use electrons to magnify specimens. This allows scientists to magnify a specimen many times more than a regular microscope would allow. Oeggl used an electron microscope to get a closer look at Ötzi's colon contents.

OEGGL INVESTIGATES ÖTZI'S COLON CONTENTS

Oeggl delicately divided his sample into four different parts so he could study them separately under an electron microscope. First he added some saline solution to rehydrate the tissue from the first piece of the sample. Then he slid it under the microscope. After adjusting the microscope to 5,000 times magnification, Oeggl took a look at Ötzi's last meal. He found many cells from the einkorn grain had tiny specks of charcoal on them, suggesting the grain had been heated in a fire. This led Oeggl to hypothesize Ötzi had eaten bread made from the tough grain.

Einkorn grain was not the only thing Oeggl observed on his first piece of sample. He also spotted grains of pollen. Oeggl knew this find meant Ötzi had at some point eaten or drunk the pollen. Pollen could provide crucial information about where Ötzi may have spent his last hours, since different plants grow at different altitudes in the Alps. To figure out which plant the pollen belonged to, Oeggl had to remove the fat and protein from the tiny sample. He used chemicals to help reveal the plant species, but the chemicals permanently altered the sample piece.

After some careful work, Oeggl had the sample ready for analysis. Once again, he slid the sample under the microscope and took a look. What he found gave him cause for concern. Most of the pollen was from hundreds of local plants. However, he also saw many bits of pollen from a plant he did not expect. His first suspicion was that the sample had been contaminated from the air and supplies in his lab, so he decided to examine the saline solution he had used to rehydrate the sample. If the sample had been contaminated, the saline solution was the most likely source. Oeggl prepared a slide of just the saline solution and slid it under the microscope. He expected to find the pollen in the saline solution; however, the saline slide was free of pollen. Oeggl was puzzled. Was it possible that this suspicious pollen had in fact come from Ötzi's colon?

Oeggl prepared the second of the four samples he had created. Once again, the pollen was present. He prepared the third and final samples. The pollen was present on them, too. Oeggl became excited. He asked his colleagues to look at the samples to confirm his findings. After they

HOP HORNBEAM

Hop hornbeam, scientific name *Ostrya carpinifolia*, is a deciduous tree found in southern Europe, western Asia, and eastern North America. It can grow approximately 50 feet (15 m) tall and has a very tough wood, which makes it ideal for use as a building material.[1] Some varieties of hop hornbeam bloom in the fall, while others, including the one that produced the pollen found in Ötzi's stomach, bloom in spring.

confirmed what Oeggl had seen, he decided to take a trip to find the tree from which the pollen came. Fortunately, he knew just where it grew.

The pollen in Ötzi's gut came from a tree called hop hornbeam, which only grows in very particular conditions. The tree needs high humidity and direct sunlight. Oeggl knew the only nearby area where this tree could have grown in these conditions was near an Italian town called Katharinaberg, which lay approximately six miles (10 km) south of the Ötztal Alps where Ötzi was discovered. The area would have also had good conditions for growing the other plant matter associated with the Iceman, such as yew, hazel, maple, and ash. Finally, Oeggl had the physical evidence he needed to make an inference about where Ötzi lived. The pollen in the Iceman's gut did not lie. Ötzi had been in the Katharinaberg area shortly before his death.

Hop hornbeam provided a clue to where Ötzi had spent the last few days before his death.

A FINAL RESTING PLACE

In January 1998, Ötzi's body was moved from the freezers in Innsbruck University to a $12 million museum created just for him in Bolzano, a city in the South Tyrol Province of Italy. The mummy had been on loan from the Italian government to Innsbruck University since the Iceman's discovery. Included in the design of the museum was a freezer designed specifically for Ötzi, according to Platzer's specifications. Not only would the freezer preserve the Iceman in glacial conditions, it would also give the world its first look at the mummy. An exhibit was designed with a small window into the freezer

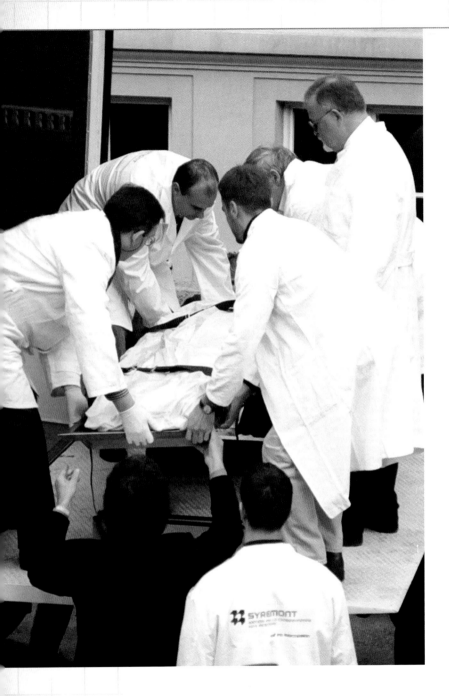

Ötzi was moved into a refrigerated crate for his journey to the new museum in South Tyrol.

so museum visitors could view the Iceman.

On January 16, 1998, Ötzi and his artifacts were driven by truck from Innsbruck University to the new museum, called the South Tyrol Museum of Archaeology. Research would now be in the control of Horst Seidler, a human biology professor from the University of Vienna who had been involved in research on the Iceman since 1991. Bruno Hosp, the cultural affairs adviser to the South Tyrol Province, had asked Seidler to take over the research once Ötzi was moved to the museum. To celebrate Ötzi's arrival, the province of South Tyrol hosted a conference featuring the scientists who had worked on the Iceman over the last seven years.

OEGGL'S THEORY

Oeggl was the last to present at the conference, and he quickly had his audience on the edges of their seats. Not all scientists had agreed with Spindler's scenario of Ötzi's death, which had been nicknamed the disaster theory. As research continued, data and theories evolved. Soon other scientists came up with new ideas and explanations surrounding the Iceman's final days.

In his presentation, Oeggl used the evidence from his hop hornbeam discovery to present an alternate theory of how Ötzi had died. Years before, Spindler had hypothesized the Iceman died in early fall after being injured when a disaster struck his community. Oeggl believed the physical evidence he had uncovered suggested a very different scenario.

Oeggl explained to his audience the variety of hop hornbeam found in Ötzi's colon only blooms in the spring. Blooming is what causes pollen to be present. Finding evidence of hop hornbeam pollen in Ötzi's colon meant the Iceman had died in early summer or late spring, not early fall as Spindler's theory asserted.

Oeggl also knew the maple leaves he found with the charcoal supported this new interpretation, though he did not share the findings with his audience because he was still conducting research. The leaves still had chlorophyll in them. Oeggl believed this meant Ötzi had pulled the leaves from trees in late spring or early summer, when leaves were green. If the leaves were collected in early fall, they would have little or no chlorophyll.

Privately, Oeggl was piecing together a new theory about the Iceman's death that would challenge the conventional thinking about the mummy. His early theory was that Ötzi was in the area near Katharinaberg hours before his death. There he had eaten his last meal and ingested the hop hornbeam pollen. He then set off up the mountain in his insulated shoes to avoid freezing in fresh snow. At some point, an accident such as a bad fall occurred, which injured Ötzi and damaged his equipment.

SOUTH TYROL MUSEUM OF ARCHAEOLOGY

On March 28, 1998, Ötzi's final resting place, the South Tyrol Museum of Archaeology, opened to the public. It has nearly 13,000 square feet (1,200 sq m) of exhibition space where visitors can view the Iceman and his belongings and learn more about the Neolithic period.[2]

MORE STUDY OF ÖTZI'S DIET

Ötzi's diet and last meal continued to be a topic of research. In 1999, a team led by Stephen Macko, a professor in the department of environmental sciences at the University of Virginia, obtained samples of Ötzi's hair for analysis. The team wanted to compare the chemical contents of the hair to that of modern vegetarians. This would help scientists determine whether or not Ötzi's diet was largely plant-based. Early study of the wear on the mummy's teeth had suggested he ate mostly plants.

Macko's team first cleaned the hair samples with distilled ethanol to remove debris and fatty acids that could possibly throw off the results. Then they analyzed the samples for stable carbon and nitrogen isotope levels, which would tell them if Ötzi's diet was largely plant-based or animal-based. They found Ötzi's levels were very similar to the levels in the hair of modern vegetarians, indicating Ötzi ate mostly plants.

A team at Innsbruck University, led by Oeggl, also took a look at Ötzi's diet. They wanted to determine whether the Iceman was omnivorous by studying the contents of the mummy's digestive tract. The team found bits of meat in Ötzi's colon as well as plant matter. Oeggl's team determined Ötzi had eaten a meal of meat, plums, wheat, and other plants before he died. These results contradicted Macko's results. It seemed the Iceman was omnivorous after all.

NEW RESEARCH SUPPORTS OEGGL'S DEATH THEORY

In 2000, a team of scientists at the Environmental Division of Arsenal Research in Vienna, Austria, conducted research that supported Oeggl's conclusions from his pollen research. Instead of plant matter, however, the team analyzed evidence of geochemicals in Ötzi's bones. Geochemicals are chemicals found in the earth's solid matter, such as rock. Geochemicals in a human body can provide evidence about where that person may have spent time. The Iceman's researchers were specifically looking at strontium and oxygen isotopes. The team took bone samples from human remains between 200 and 800 years old from the area in which the Iceman was found and compared them against samples of Ötzi's bone.

The Arsenal Research team found the levels of strontium and oxygen isotopes in Ötzi's bones were very similar to those in the samples from the other remains, indicating he lived in the Ötztal or Vinschgau regions of the Alps, near Katharinaberg. The team incorporated Oeggl's pollen research into their results, inferring Ötzi traveled between the Ötztal and Vinschgau valleys

Geochemicals analyzed in 2000 identified the Iceman as a resident of the Ötztal Valley near where he was found.

through a mountain pass. The Iceman may have died while on a trip between the two.

The Arsenal Research team's findings also helped support a new theory being considered among leading Ötzi scientists, including Oeggl. The team found evidence in Ötzi's bones that he had been submerged under cold water for months, which would have prompted the first stage of mummification—converting fat into adipocere, a soapy, greasy substance of fatty acids created by the activity of anaerobic bacteria in a wet environment. A few years earlier, Oeggl had begun to suspect the Iceman had not necessarily died on the boulder where the Simons found him.

> **"Gradually, we have to take leave of the idea that the spot on which [Ötzi] was discovered is the same spot on which he died."[3]**
> —KLAUS OEGGL, CHALLENGING CONVENTIONAL WISDOM ABOUT ÖTZI'S DEATH IN 1998

Oeggl believed Ötzi had died elsewhere, and glacial movement in the 5,300 years between his death and discovery planted him where he had been found. The site maps from Lippert's digs supported this idea. Ötzi's artifacts were found strewn about the site, not in a concentrated area, as they would have been if the Iceman had died at his campsite. Hairline fractures zur Nedden and Seidler found on Ötzi's

Oeggl argued the Ötztal Alps' glaciers were responsible for transporting the Iceman's body.

skull could have been caused by natural freezing and thawing of glacial ice and snow. The Arsenal Research team's study seemed to support the idea that Ötzi had been in water before being frozen in ice. Could that water have moved him from where he died to where he was found? Nearly a decade after his discovery, the Iceman continued to confound and surprise scientists.

6

A Surprising Find

In late spring 2001, the lab of Italian radiologist Paul Gostner was abuzz with a new find that would change the narrative of Ötzi's death. Gostner and his team at the Regional General Hospital in Bolzano had compiled all the X-ray and CT scans taken of the Iceman since research began in 1991— 2,190 in all.[1] The team's goal was to scrutinize the photos to see what Ötzi's bones and tissues could show them about his life and health.

At the South Tyrol Museum of Archaeology, Ötzi is housed in a specially designed freezer intended to preserve the mummy.

Gostner was analyzing an X-ray of Ötzi's ribs and shoulder blades when he noticed a strange white spot. Finding such a spot on an X-ray image indicates to radiologists that something is partially blocking the X-rays from passing through the object or person being X-rayed. For example, bones appear white on an X-ray image because they partially block X-rays. However, this white spot was not a bone.

To find out what the spot could be, Gostner took a second look at more detailed CT scans of the same area. What he found was unexpected. An arrowhead was lodged between Ötzi's left shoulder blade and his rib cage. Upon closer inspection, Gostner and his team determined the arrow had penetrated so

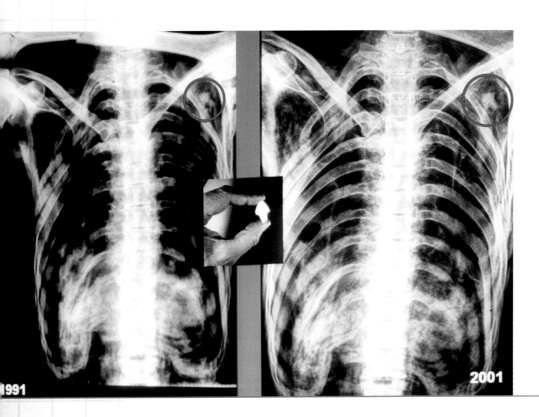

1991

2001

X-rays taken of Ötzi's chest show an arrowhead lodged there.

deeply into the Iceman's torso that it would have nicked a major blood vessel. The team hypothesized that Ötzi would have died from a loss of blood due to the wound.

After finding the arrowhead on the images, the team wanted to confirm its presence by finding a puncture wound on Ötzi's back. They found a small laceration over his left shoulder blade. It was the evidence the team was looking for. It seemed the Iceman had been shot in the back with an arrow. Gostner and his team considered the Iceman may have somehow fallen on the arrow. However, they believed another explanation was much more likely—murder. It would take a few more years of research, however, to fully understand the wounds that contributed to Ötzi's death.

AGONIZING ARROWHEAD

The arrowhead Gostner found lodged between Ötzi's left shoulder blade and rib cage was made of flint. This hard, dark quartz rock was used to create weapons or to light fires in prehistoric cultures. As they studied the X-rays and the site on the Iceman's skin where the arrow entered his body, scientists were able to determine the arrow left a hole nearly one inch (2 cm) wide in the mummy's left shoulder blade.[2] Scientists came to hypothesize that the heavy bleeding from the wound would have caused paralysis in the Iceman's left arm.

ADDITIONAL DISCOVERIES

Finding the arrowhead was not the only outcome of Gostner's research. His team uncovered interesting findings from Ötzi's head all the way down to his toes. As zur Nedden had before them, they noticed many hairline fractures on the skull, including in the facial area. The scientists hypothesized these fractures had been caused by glacial ice and snow moving over the body and pushing it around. The Iceman's teeth also provided new information. Most were worn down and flattened from use. The researchers believe this wear was not only from eating tough foods like einkorn bread but also from Ötzi using his teeth as tools to tear leather or perform other tasks.

Analysis of images of Ötzi's spine and torso revealed evidence of disease and trauma. Gostner's team also found evidence of hardened arteries, as the Innsbruck researchers had noted. This was an indicator of heart disease. The discovery was a surprise for scientists. Most scientists considered heart disease to be a modern disease caused by lifestyle, tobacco use, and diet. This find suggested humans had been at risk for heart disease much earlier than scientists had thought probable.

As they examined Ötzi's spine, Gostner's team found evidence of arthritis, an inflammatory condition, which would have plagued Ötzi's hip joints. This corroborated the findings of earlier studies. The condition would have been painful for Ötzi. Lastly, Gostner examined CT scans and X-rays of the Iceman's chest taken several years earlier. These revealed several broken ribs, as zur Nedden had originally noted. Some ribs showed evidence of being well healed; others had not healed at all. The healed bones suggested injuries that had occurred well before Ötzi met his death. The unhealed bones pointed to injuries just prior to death or after he had perished.

Gostner and his team made another interesting discovery. While the team explained that finding an exact age for Ötzi was nearly impossible, they hypothesized that the Iceman was between 40 and 50 years old when he died, at least ten years older than previously thought. Gostner's team based this inference on bone evidence of Ötzi's active, Alpine lifestyle. Parts of his bones were thicker, indicating a more active younger adult, while arthritis and calcification on other bones indicated the Iceman was older, perhaps even in his 60s. The team cut the difference and reasoned Ötzi died when he was between 40 and 50 years of age.

"WISPS OF TISSUE"

In its study of the X-ray and CT scan images, Gostner's team was able to see Ötzi's tissues as well as his bones. However, the team found most of Ötzi's organs were shrunken, often to the point that scientists could barely identify them. For example, Ötzi's lungs were so dehydrated scientists described them as "wisps of tissue" on the X-ray and CT scans.[3] In addition to the lungs, the team also found Ötzi's liver and bowel.

SPINNING CENTRIFUGE

A centrifuge is a piece of equipment researchers use to separate DNA from the rest of a sample of organic matter, using centrifugal force. This force causes the parts of a spinning object to move outward from the rotation's center. When a centrifuge is used to separate DNA, it is called centrifugation. A centrifuge uses centrifugal forces to spin samples so quickly the different substances in the samples separate by particle size and density. After it is spun in a centrifuge, the DNA in a sample can be extracted from the top layer, called the plasmid.

DNA ANALYSIS OF ÖTZI'S COLON CONTENTS

In 2002, a team of researchers from Italy's University of Camerino extracted DNA from two tiny samples of the contents of Ötzi's colon and ileum, a part of the small intestine. The samples were soaked in a solution overnight. Then researchers ground them up. These steps prepared the samples to be put through a centrifuge to separate the DNA from the rest of the matter in the sample.

Once the DNA of the food samples had been separated, the team compared the results with an international database maintained by the National Center for Biotechnology Information. The samples returned evidence that the Iceman had eaten plant, fungus, and animal matter before he died. The DNA of the plant contents in his colon were 73 percent pine tree, 22 percent cereals—such as einkorn—and 5 percent ferns.[4] The team inferred that pollen and spores likely accounted for the pine and fern DNA. The

DNA of the contents in Ötzi's ileum indicated he ate cereals prior to his death.

The researchers also found evidence Ötzi had ingested fungi, but the scientists thought the fungus may have appeared on Ötzi's corpse after he was trapped in the ice. They also found that though the Iceman had eaten ibex meat before he died, his last meal was actually red deer. From their research, the scientists hypothesized that Ötzi was a hunter and warrior, making a journey through a pine forest after eating a meal of ibex and plants. Then, he died shortly after he had another meal of red deer meat and some cereals.

CHEMICALS SHED MORE LIGHT ON ÖTZI'S HOMELAND

In 2003, a team of scientists from Australia, Germany, and the United States took a look at the geochemicals in Ötzi's body and equipment.

After studying the Iceman's colon and ileum, researchers concluded he was likely a hunter.

DIGGING
DEEPER

A Wounded Hand

In 2003, a group of German and Italian pathologists and other scientists published a study about their analysis of Ötzi's right hand. The team had discovered a deep stab wound that ran across Ötzi's right palm between his thumb and index finger, finally stopping on the back of his hand.

To confirm chemically what they observed visually, the scientists ran samples of the wounded tissues through some chemical tests. They rehydrated the sample using a staining chemical that would give off light if blood were present. The team found evidence of a blood clot in the sample from the wound site. Further analysis determined the wound would have been three to eight days old at the time of the Iceman's

Ötzi may have received his hand injury while defending himself from an attacker.

death. Now, scientists needed to determine how Ötzi was injured. Was the wound the result of an accident or a physical conflict with another person?

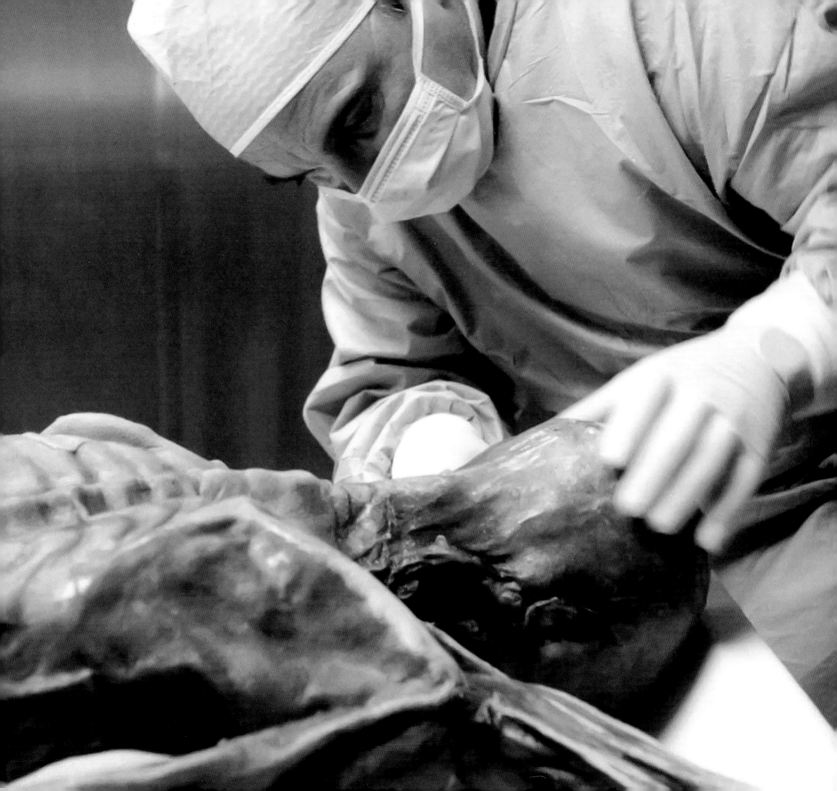

7

Recent Developments

As the twentieth anniversary of Ötzi's discovery approached, scientists continued studying the mummy in an effort to learn more about his death, his last days, and his culture. Since the library of research on the Iceman had grown quite large since 1991, new studies often focused on expanding, confirming, or refuting past scientific work.

Ötzi's researchers continue uncovering surprising finds and developing new hypotheses and theories surrounding the Iceman's last days.

ÖTZI'S NEW LOOK

To celebrate the twentieth anniversary of Ötzi's discovery, the South Tyrol Museum of Archaeology unveiled a new 3-D model of the Iceman. Created by Dutch artists Alfons and Adrie Kennis, the realistic-looking sculpture was conceived using 3-D scans of the mummy's body. The new model shows an aged man with wrinkles looking over his left shoulder.

NEW SCRUTINY OF ÖTZI'S LAST MEAL

In 2005, German biological anthropologist Albert Zink and a team of scientists took some new CT scan images of Ötzi's torso and turned up a surprising new discovery: the Iceman's stomach. Until then, scientists had looked for the organ where it usually rests—on the left side of a person's upper abdomen. However, the new images revealed Ötzi's stomach had shrunk and moved farther up into Ötzi's upper abdomen, where no one had thought to look. Furthermore, it seemed the stomach had something in it.

The new discovery prompted Zink's team to extract a sample of the Iceman's stomach contents in November 2005. An early analysis of the DNA of the contents revealed Ötzi's last meal had been ibex meat, not red deer as the 2002 study had suggested, and some plant matter. Oeggl was charged with analyzing the plant samples. The stomach findings provided more evidence the Iceman ate both animals and plants, not primarily plants.

MORE DETAILS ON ÖTZI'S MORTAL WOUND

Since Gostner's discovery of the arrowhead in 2001, popular opinion about Ötzi's death had shifted from assuming the prehistoric man died from injuries sustained in an accident to murder. Most assumed the wound from the arrow puncture had caused the Iceman to perish.

In 2007, a team of scientists led by Frank Rühli of the Institute of Anatomy at the University of Zurich in Switzerland took new X-rays of the area where the arrowhead penetrated Ötzi's torso. As past research found, the arrow had traveled through Ötzi's shoulder blade, lodging itself in the Iceman's torso and nicking an artery. The new X-ray found new evidence confirming the mortal damage to the artery. The image revealed a one-half-inch- (1.3 cm) long cut on the artery and blood clotting in Ötzi's tissue around the cut.[1] Researchers asserted this injury would have

SHOT FROM BEHIND . . . AND FROM BELOW?

In the wake of the revelations about Ötzi's death, in 2007 Gostner and Lippert offered a new hypothesis of what had happened up on the mountain. The scientists theorized the evidence suggested the Iceman was shot in the back by an assailant who was standing farther down the mountain than he was. Gostner and Lippert believed Ötzi fell down after being wounded, hit his head on a rock, and landed on his back. Then, they theorized, his attacker flipped him over, removed the arrow shaft, and left the Iceman's body on the side of the mountain.

caused the Iceman to bleed out and that his heart likely stopped only a few minutes after he was shot due to this blood loss.

One of Rühli's colleagues was Eduard Egarter Vigl, the director for the Institute of Pathology at the Central Hospital in Bolzano, the same hospital where radiologist Gostner worked. After the results of the study were in, Egarter Vigl offered some new insights on Ötzi's death. The team had noticed the arrow shaft from the fatal arrowhead had never been found at the site of Ötzi's discovery. They asserted the Iceman's attacker must have tried to pull the arrow out of Ötzi's back after shooting him, leaving the arrowhead but not the shaft.

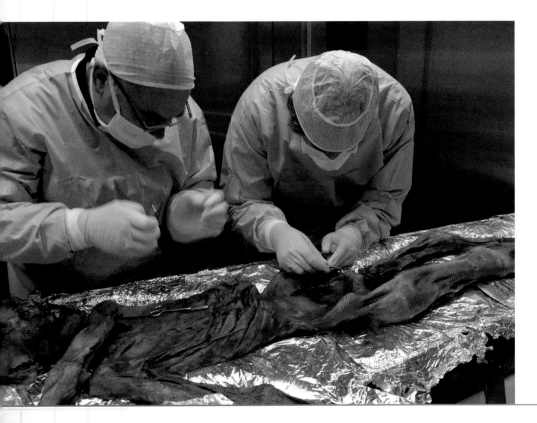

Eduard Egarter Vigl, *left*, and Albert Zink, *right*, examined Ötzi in 2010.

Egarter Vigl provided an explanation for this seemingly bizarre behavior. Since all Neolithic hunters had to make their own ammunition, it would have been possible for Ötzi's attacker to be identified by his arrow if it had been left in the corpse. Egarter Vigl believed the attacker was trying to keep his identity secret by taking the arrow with him. This hypothesis would also explain why the attacker had left the Iceman's valuable copper-headed ax behind—taking it would have identified him as the killer.

DID HEAD TRAUMA CAUSE ÖTZI'S DEMISE?

Just a month after Rühli's research was announced, a team of researchers from the newly developed Institute for Mummies and the Iceman, led by Zink, offered new evidence the arrow may not have been entirely responsible for Ötzi's death.

Zink's team had taken a closer look at some of the images from Rühli's research on the arrowhead wound. Instead of focusing on the shoulder blade, however, Zink's team analyzed X-ray images of Ötzi's skull. They found the Iceman was the victim of severe head trauma. Previously, fractures on Ötzi's skull were thought to be the product of glacial snow and ice moving over the corpse. However, Zink's team found evidence the brain had been injured by the breaks, indicating Ötzi was alive before suffering the skull fractures.

KLAUS OEGGL

Klaus Oeggl spent at least a decade of his career engaged in studying Ötzi. As a young assistant professor of botany in the Institute of Botany of Innsbruck University, Oeggl's knowledge of paleobotany and his enthusiasm impressed Ötzi's research leaders, which led to his participation in research on the mummy. Years later, Oeggl continued contributing valuable research about the Iceman's diet, where he lived, and even how he died. His contributions to Ötzi research helped improve the scientific world's understanding of prehistoric humans.

This replica of a Neolithic house in Italy may be similar to the type of dwelling Ötzi lived in.

mummy. The pouch contained an awl made of bone, two blades, and a blade-sharpening tool created from the wood of a lime tree and a deer antler. All the contents were created from regional materials harvested from plants and animals.

Another aspect of Oeggl's study focused once more on Ötzi's colon contents and what they could tell scientists about the Iceman's habitat and time of death. The plant matter in his colon confirmed Ötzi lived in a southern, lower-altitude habitat rather than up on the mountain closer to where he was discovered. In fact, Oeggl concluded, the evidence suggested a settlement in an Alpine valley near the Inn and Etsch valleys of northern Italy.

A CONTROVERSIAL NEW NARRATIVE

In 2010, scientists from Italy's Sapienza University in Rome, led by archaeologist Alessandro Vanzetti, published a study that challenged the murder theory now largely embraced by the scientific community. The new study asserted Ötzi was killed at a low altitude—not up on the mountain— then taken up the mountain with his belongings to be buried by his family members when spring snows melted. The team supported its hypothesis by pointing to how Ötzi's items were distributed on the mountain. Vanzetti's team argued that Ötzi's family put him on a stone platform approximately

16 feet (5 m) uphill from where Ötzi was found in 1991.[4] Over time, glacial movement swept the mummy and his belongings down to their final resting place, scattering his equipment.

Shortly after it was published, scientists at the South Tyrol Museum of Archaeology refuted Vanzetti's hypothesis. The museum's scientists claimed the idea that Ötzi's family held onto his body until the snow melted in the spring, then buried him, was inconsistent with how much the body had decomposed before it was encased in ice for thousands of years.

TWENTIETH ANNIVERSARY CONFERENCE

Between October 20 and 22, 2011, the European Academy of Bolzano hosted a conference of approximately 100 experts to celebrate the twentieth anniversary of the Iceman's discovery. At the conference, scientists seemed to reach a new consensus about the circumstances surrounding Ötzi's death. Oeggl's research was one of the highlights of the meeting. First, he and two Austrian scientists once again argued against the earlier hypothesis that the Iceman was a herdsman bringing his herd down from the mountains in early fall when he fell victim to some disaster. Oeggl's 1996 research on the pollen contents of Ötzi's colon was confirmed by new evidence of hop hornbeam in Ötzi's stomach contents, proving the man had ingested the pollen shortly before he died.

Zink also revealed the entire contents of Ötzi's stomach at the conference. The Iceman's last meal had been of ibex meat, einkorn, leaves, apples, and some flies' wings. Lastly, researchers from the University of Munich, in Germany, presented new evidence that the head wound Ötzi suffered would have been enough to kill him, even without the mortal arrow wound.

It is probable ibex was one of Ötzi's final meals.

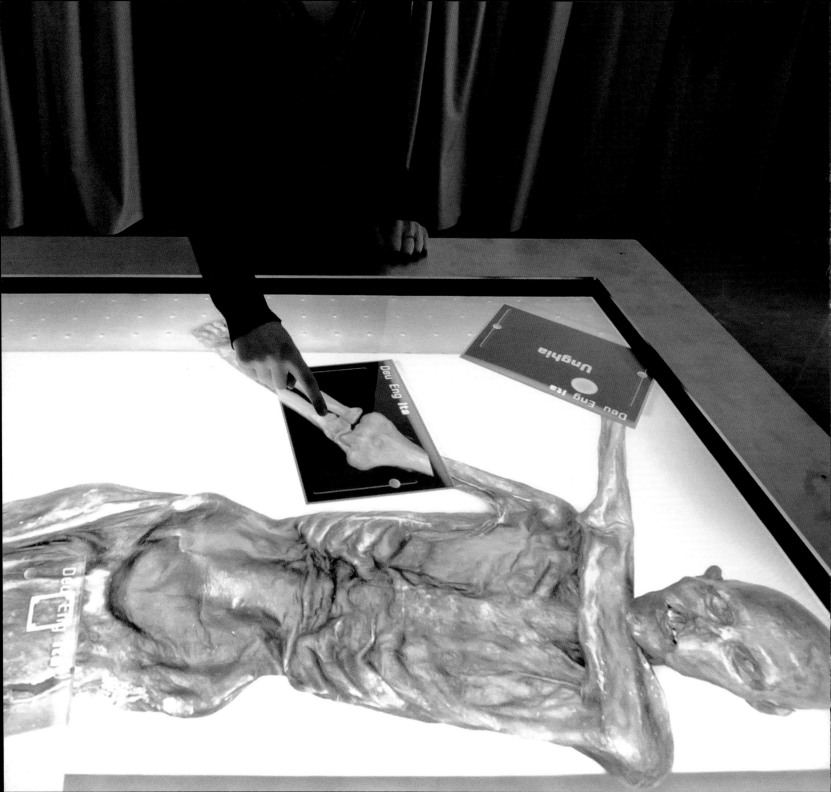

Reflecting on the Research

More than two decades of research conducted on Ötzi so far has helped scientists and the people of the world understand their heritage as humans. Learning more about Ötzi and others in his society helps present-day scientists, students, and the public make connections between prehistoric and modern humans.

A 2011 exhibit at the South Tyrol Museum of Archaeology allowed visitors to learn more about the research conducted on Ötzi.

HOMO SAPIENS

Modern-day humans and humans in Ötzi's time belong to the same species—*Homo sapiens*. Homo sapiens evolved in Africa approximately 200,000 years ago and then migrated to other parts of the world. Homo sapiens have light body builds and larger brains than earlier species of humans. To accommodate their big brains, Homo sapiens' skulls gradually changed shape to become high vaulted, with a flat forehead that is nearly vertical and shows little sign of the heavy brow found in other species of ancient humans.

UNCOVERING ÖTZI'S MODERN RELATIVES

In 2012, Zink and his colleagues at the Institute for Mummies and the Iceman announced some novel findings regarding Ötzi's DNA. In 2008, Ötzi's entire genome had been sequenced, giving scientists a large amount of data to analyze. One of the first studies looked into Ötzi's heritage and the possibility of existing modern relatives. The researchers found Ötzi's mtDNA contained mutations not found in the modern human genome. This discovery led scientists to believe Ötzi's society had since gone extinct. However, some mutations on the Iceman's Y chromosome, passed down by his father, were similar to those still found in men from Corsica and Sardinia, islands in the Mediterranean Sea.

During the Neolithic period, people from the Middle East migrated north into Europe, including Central Europe and the islands in the Mediterranean Sea. While these migrants eventually intermixed with people in mainland Europe, those on the islands, including Sardinia and Corsica, were more isolated and did not mix nearly as much. This led to the modern populations of Sardinia and Corsica having more genetic traces of prehistoric populations than those in modern Central Europe.

In addition to revelations regarding the Iceman's genetic heritage, his DNA sequence provided some answers about the prehistoric man's physical features and even the diseases he suffered from. Ötzi was an athletic man with brown eyes and type O blood. He was lactose intolerant, which meant his body could not process the sugars in dairy. He also suffered from Lyme disease, an infection transmitted by ticks that causes fever, headaches, and even heart and neurological problems. In fact, Ötzi contains the oldest known trace of the illness.

At the Ötzi Village in Umhausen, archaeologists have created replicas of homes similar to the ones humans may have lived in during Ötzi's time.

discoveries was that the Iceman suffered from heart disease. Until that revelation, scientists believed heart disease was a modern affliction caused by diets full of rich foods, sedentary lifestyles, and tobacco use. In the Iceman, scientists also found the oldest trace of Lyme disease and proof that prehistoric joints suffered from arthritis, as do many modern humans'. Beyond physiology lies a deeper connection. The Iceman's DNA sequence links him to people living today on the Mediterranean islands of Sardinia and Corsica.

Research on Ötzi has provided a wealth of information about humans living in the Neolithic period. In fact, dating the mummy has changed scientists' understanding of the timeline of human development. Before finding the Iceman and his copper-headed ax, archaeologists thought humans in Central Europe had not learned the art and science of smelting copper until approximately 2000 BCE. Ötzi and his

"There were frequent innovations, changes, progressive developments and surely also reverses over the nearly 4,000 years of the Neolithic period. Man was constantly on the road of progress—whatever his goal. The archaeologist can confirm such changes even on the strength of his usually scant source material, albeit only intermittently and by inference."[2]

—KONRAD SPINDLER DISCUSSING THE NEOLITHIC PERIOD IN HIS BOOK THE MAN IN THE ICE, 1994

belongings moved this date 1,000 years earlier.

A NEW EXHIBIT

In January 2013, the South Tyrol Museum of Archaeology unveiled a brand-new, permanent exhibit dedicated to Ötzi and his belongings. The exhibit was based on a special exhibit created to celebrate the Iceman's twentieth anniversary in 2011. In addition to the updated Ötzi exhibit, the museum also installed space for showcasing other unique finds from the region. The new exhibits guarantee Ötzi not only a prominent place in archaeological science but also in the hearts and minds of people around the world.

Scientists may never fully unravel the secrets of Ötzi's life and mysterious death, but people's fascination with the Iceman continues.

TIMELINE

1991

On September 19, Erika and Helmut Simon discover Ötzi while hiking in the Alps.

1991

Ötzi is extracted from the ice on September 23.

1991

In December, radiocarbon dating of grass samples found near Ötzi reveals the mummy is 5,300 years old.

1992

In July, Andreas Lippert's team uncovers more than 400 specimens from Ötzi's discovery site.

1993

The first analysis of Ötzi's DNA reveals Ötzi was a resident of the area around the Ötztal Valley.

1996

Klaus Oeggl's analysis of Ötzi's colon contents reveals he traveled farther south than scientists previously thought.

1998

In January, Ötzi is moved from Innsbruck University to the new South Tyrol Museum of Archaeology.

2001

In spring, Paul Gostner finds an arrowhead lodged between Ötzi's rib cage and left shoulder blade.

2003

German and Italian scientists discover a deep wound on Ötzi's right hand.

2007

A Swiss team finds the cut on Ötzi's artery caused by the arrowhead; Albert Zink's team uncovers evidence of a serious head wound that could have contributed to Ötzi's death.

2011

From October 20 to 22, a conference is held in honor of the twentieth anniversary of Ötzi's discovery.

2013

The South Tyrol Museum of Archaeology opens a permanent exhibit dedicated to Ötzi and his belongings in January.

ADDITIONAL RESOURCES

SELECTED BIBLIOGRAPHY

Fowler, Brenda. *Iceman: Uncovering the Life and Times of a Prehistoric Man Found in an Alpine Glacier.* New York: Random, 2000. Print.

Spindler, Konrad. *The Man in the Ice: The Discovery of a 5,000-Year-Old Body Reveals the Secrets of the Stone Age.* New York: Harmony, 1994. Print.

FURTHER READINGS

Deem, James M. *Bodies from the Ice: Melting Glaciers and the Recovery of the Past.* Boston: Houghton Mifflin, 2008. Print.

Down, David. *The Archaeology Book.* Green Forest, AR: Master, 2010. Print.

Sloan, Christopher. *Mummies: Dried, Tanned, Sealed, Drained, Frozen, Embalmed, Stuffed, Wrapped, and Smoked . . . and We're Dead Serious.* Washington, DC: National Geographic, 2010. Print.

WEBSITES

To learn more about Digging Up the Past, visit **booklinks.abdopublishing.com**. These links are routinely monitored and updated to provide the most current information available.

Chapter 7. Recent Developments

1. John Roach. "Iceman Bled Out from Arrow Wound, X-Ray Scan Reveals." *Daily News*. National Geographic Society, 7 June 2007. Web. 14 June 2013.

2. Klaus Oeggl, et al. "The Reconstruction of the Last Itinerary of 'Ötzi,' the Neolithic Iceman, by Pollen Analyses from Sequentially Sampled Gut Extracts." *Quaternary Science Reviews* 26.6–7 (2007): 853–861. Science Direct. Web. 13 June 2013.

3. Ibid.

4. Bruce Bower. "Study Alters Cold Case Death Theory." *Science News* 25 Sept. 2010: 14. *JSTOR*. Web. 12 June 2013.

Chapter 8. Reflecting on the Research

1. *Iceman Murder Mystery*. Nova. PBS Video, 2011. Web. 15 May 2013.

2. Konrad Spindler. *The Man in the Ice: The Discovery of a 5,000-Year-Old Body Reveals the Secrets of the Stone Age*. New York: Harmony, 1994. Print. 188.

INDEX

ABOUT THE AUTHOR

Amanda Lanser is a freelance writer who lives in Minneapolis, Minnesota. She and her husband are animal lovers and have two cats, Quigley and Aveh, and a greyhound, Laila. Amanda enjoys writing books for kids of all ages and remembers reading about Ötzi the Iceman when she was a student.